Ancient Egyptian GEOGRAPHY

Leigh Rockwood

Published in 2014 by The Rosen Publishing Group, Inc.
29 East 21st Street, New York, NY 10010

First Edition

Editor: Jennifer Way
Book Design: Kate Vlachos
Layout Design: Colleen Bialecki

Photo Credits: Cover AR/Getty Images; p. 4 Kaarsten/Shutterstock.com; p. 5 Bart Acke/ Shutterstock.com; p. 6 Michael Benanav/Lonely Planet Images/Getty Images; pp. 7, 10, 12, 14, 17, 20 DEA Picture Library/Getty Images; p. 8 Werner Forman/Universal Images Group/ Getty Images; p. 9 © 2001 Francis Dzikowski; p. 11 iStockphoto/Thinkstock; p. 13 Oleg Kozlov/Shutterstock.com; p. 15 Sylvain Grandadam/The Image Bank/Getty Images; p. 15 (bottom) BasPhoto/Shutterstock.com; p. 16 Antonio Abrignani/Shutterstock.com; p. 18 Egyptian 18th Dynasty/The Bridgeman Art Library/Getty Images; p. 19 Teerawut/Shutterstock.com; p. 21 Hisham Ibrahim/Photographer's Choice/Getty Images; p. 22 Strakovskaya/Shutterstock.com.

Library of Congress Cataloging-in-Publication Data

Rockwood, Leigh.
Ancient Egyptian geography / by Leigh Rockwood. — First edition.
pages cm. — (Spotlight on ancient civilizations: Egypt)
Includes index.
ISBN 978-1-4777-0767-8 (library binding) — ISBN 978-1-4777-0867-5 (pbk.) — ISBN 978-1-4777-0868-2 (6-pack)
1. Geography—Egypt–History—Juvenile literature. 2. Geography, Ancient—Juvenile literature. I. Title.
GB332.R63 2014
913.2—dc23

2013001129

Manufactured in the United States of America

CPSIA Compliance Information: Batch #S13PK2: For Further Information contact Rosen Publishing, New York, New York at 1-800-237-9932

CONTENTS

The Geography of Ancient Egypt

The ancient Egyptian **civilization** was heavily influenced by its geography. People settled along the land on either side of the Nile River. They also settled in the Nile **Delta**. This is a wide, triangular area in Egypt's north where the Nile River branches out as it gets closer to the Mediterranean Sea. The lands in these areas were the most **fertile** in Egypt.

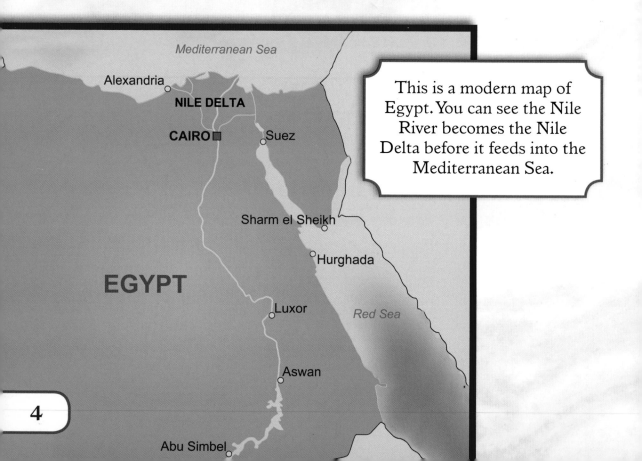

Mediterranean Sea

Alexandria

NILE DELTA

CAIRO ■   Suez

This is a modern map of Egypt. You can see the Nile River becomes the Nile Delta before it feeds into the Mediterranean Sea.

EGYPT

Sharm el Sheikh

Hurghada

Luxor   Red Sea

Aswan

4

Abu Simbel

The Nile River forms the backbone of modern day Egypt. These sailboats are on the Nile in the city of Aswan, Egypt.

Beyond these fertile lands surrounding the Nile were deserts. The Arabian Desert lay to the east and the Libyan Desert lay to the west. People did not settle in these hot, dry lands.

Ancient Egypt's Two Lands

Ancient Egyptians divided their land into two main regions. The land surrounding the Nile River was called Kemet. This name meant "black land," after the rich dark soil left behind by the Nile's yearly flooding. Kemet was where crops were planted and where most ancient Egyptians lived.

The term Desheret, or "red land," referred both to the reddish color of the sand as well as the heat of the sun. This photo shows the Libyan Desert in western Egypt.

This tomb painting shows workers in the field in Kemet, the fertile "black land."

The desert that surrounded Kemet was called Desheret. This name meant "red land." Ancient Egyptians hunted animals and mined stone for their temples and tombs in Desheret. Desheret was also where ancient Egyptians buried their dead.

The Nile River

Ancient Egyptians depended on the Nile River. It provided water for farming and raising animals. The fish that lived in its waters provided food. A shipbuilding **industry** was also centered on the Nile. These ships were used to move goods between towns.

The Nile was full of fish, such as tilapia. Tilapia were so plentiful that they stood for new life to ancient Egyptians. This painted glass jar from around 1350 BC is in the shape of a tilapia.

This tomb painting shows people hunting along the Nile. Ancient Egyptians hunted for birds such as ducks and geese, as well as other game.

The Nile's yearly floods left behind rich soil along its banks. This soil made it possible to grow crops in Egypt. Ancient Egyptians created a calendar to keep track of the Nile's flooding, so that they knew the best time to plant their crops. The flooding season began in what we call June and lasted until October. Then they planted their crops, which would begin to be harvested in February.

9

Life in the Desert

As it does today, ancient Egypt had a hot and dry desert **climate**. The power of the Sun's rays fascinated ancient Egyptians. The Sun was so important that it was part of their religion in the form of Ra, the Sun god. Ra was **worshipped** as one of the ancient Egyptian religion's most important gods.

The Sun god Ra was often shown with the head of a falcon and with a sun disk over his head. Here the sun disk is giving off rays of light in the form of lotus flowers.

The pharaoh Akhenaton (center) is shown worshipping Aten. Aten is the sun disk separated from the Sun god Ra. Akhenaton tried to make the worship of Aten a new religion, but it did not last.

During the summer, a daytime temperature of around 100° F (38° C) was common, although the temperature cooled after sunset. During the winter, daytime temperatures were around 65° F (18° C).

Geography and Technology

The ancient Egyptian **empire** is one of the world's oldest civilizations. People first began settling along the Nile thousands of years ago. Two separate kingdoms eventually developed along the Nile. These kingdoms were first **unified**, or brought together, as an empire around 3100 BC.

This painting shows a man drawing water from an irrigation system so that he can water crops.

This photograph shows an irrigation canal in modern day Egypt. The water from this canal can then be directed to farmland.

Ancient Egyptians developed **technology** to make better use of the Nile's waters. To control the flow of the river's waters, they built dams, canals, and **irrigation** systems. That way the water flowed to where it was needed for farming. Such building projects encouraged the growth of cities along the Nile and the spread of Egypt's civilization along with it.

13

Agriculture in Ancient Egypt

Agriculture was the main industry in ancient Egypt. Farm animals were raised for their milk, meat, and skins. Goats, sheep, cows, and pigs were a few common farm animals.

This painting shows people harvesting grain. Grains, such as wheat and barley, were used for food as well as brewed into beer.

Left: Grain crops are still grown in Egypt today.
Below: This carving on a temple wall shows a person making an offering from the wheat harvest to the gods.

Major crops included barley, flax, and wheat. Flax was used to make a cloth called linen. Barley and wheat were grown to make both bread and beer. Other common food crops included cucumbers, dates, grapes, and melons. Papyrus, a plant that grew along the Nile, was harvested to make the paper used by ancient Egyptians.

Farming the Land

Ancient Egyptians used simple farming tools to work the land. They used hoes to break up the dirt and to dig irrigation canals. Plows were used to prepare the ground for planting seeds. Sometimes cattle were used to pull the plows.

This drawing from the 1840s shows how shadufs were used to carry loads of water in ancient Egypt.

This sickle was used to cut grain crops in ancient Egypt.

A shaduf was a tool used to carry water to the fields. This tool was made up of a pole with a bucket on one end and a weight on the other end. When the bucket was filled with water the weight helped a person balance the pole. This helped a person to more easily carry a heavy load of water.

Egypt's Natural Resources

Mud from the Nile's banks was an important natural resource for ancient Egyptians. The mud was used to make bricks for buildings. It was also used to make pottery used for cooking and storage.

Gold was commonly made into jewelry, like this necklace from the tomb of the pharaoh Tutankhamen.

Temples were often decorated with statues honoring pharaohs, like the one shown here.

Egypt's deserts held valuable natural resources, too. Desert stone was used to build tombs, temples, and statues. Metals, such as gold, were found in the mountains in Egypt's east and southeast. These metals were used to make weapons, tools, and jewelry. They were also important for trade with other kingdoms that had resources that Egypt lacked, such as wood.

Protected by Desert

Ancient Egypt's deserts were not good for agriculture. However, the surrounding deserts played an important part in protecting the empire. The lack of water, the heat, and the fierce animals, such as cobras and lions, made the Arabian and Libyan deserts dangerous to cross.

Fierce animals, such as lions, once lived at the edges of Egypt's deserts. Ancient Egyptians thought of them as guardians of their kingdom. Carvings like this one often decorated tombs.

Alexander the Great was the Greek leader who conquered Egypt in 332 BC.

There were other natural **barriers** that protected Egypt. There was the Mediterranean Sea to the north, the Red Sea to the east, and swamps to the south. The Hyksos, the Assyrians, and the Persians all interrupted Egypt's empire for short periods of time, though. Even so, the ancient Egyptian civilization lasted almost 3,000 years before it was taken over by the Greeks in 332 BC.

Made Possible by the Nile

Civilizations are formed by people, but their growth is often heavily influenced by the geography that surrounds them. Ancient Egypt was made possible by its geography. Without the Nile River, the land would have been a desert unable to support people living there. Without the protection of the deserts and seas that bordered it, ancient Egypt might have been easier for enemies to attack and would not have had a chance to flourish as it did for nearly 3,000 years.

This drawing on papyrus shows the pharaoh floating along the Nile River. The river is filled with fish and has papyrus plants growing on its banks. The things shown in this drawing were all important to ancient Egyptians.

GLOSSARY

agriculture (A-grih-kul-cher) The science of producing crops and raising livestock, or animals.

barriers (BAR-ee-erz) Something that blocks something else from passing.

civilization (sih-vih-lih-ZAY-shun) People living in an organized way.

climate (KLY-mut) The kind of weather a certain place has.

delta (DEL-tuh) A pile of earth and sand that collects at the mouth of a river.

empire (EM-pyr) A large area controlled by one ruler.

fertile (FER-tul) Good for making and growing things.

industry (IN-dus-tree) A business in which many people work and make money producing a product.

irrigation (ih-rih-GAY-shun) The carrying of water to land through ditches or pipes.

technology (tek-NAH-luh-jee) The way that people do something using tools and the tools that they use.

tombs (TOOMZ) Graves.

unified (YOO-nih-fyd) Joined together.

worshipped (WUR-shupd) To pay great honor and respect to something or someone.

INDEX

WEBSITES

Due to the changing nature of Internet links, PowerKids Press has developed an online list of websites related to the subject of this book. This site is updated regularly. Please use this link to access the list: www.powerkidslinks.com/sace/geo/